AZTEC LIFE

Who Were the Aztecs?

We call them the Aztecs because they claimed to have come from Aztlan, northwest of present-day Mexico City. But this wandering, warlike group called themselves the Mexica (*Mesheeca*). They invaded the Valley of Mexico in about A.D. 1100. Believing they were guided by their god Huitzilopochtli ("Hummingbird God of the Left"), the early Aztecs traveled around looking for a home. Finally they settled in Tenochtitlan, where Mexico City is today. Within 200 years they had taken control of the whole valley. At its height in 1519, the Aztec Empire spread over about 125,000 sq miles (200,000 sq km). At least three million people, who spoke more than 20 different languages, lived under Aztec rule. Grand pyramids rose in Tenochtitlan, one of the most beautiful cities in the world.

A WELCOME SIGN

The Mexica were nomads for many years. In about 1325, they saw the sign their priest had foretold. On an island in a large lake, they saw an eagle on a cactus eating a snake. The eagle was a symbol of the life-giving sun. The cactus stood for the human sacrifices the god needed to keep the sun coming up each day.

REWRITING HISTORY

Izcoatl, the first Aztec ruler, wanted his people to be known for greatness. So he destroyed all the writings that said the Aztecs had been rough wanderers. He admired the Toltecs, an advanced people who had died out. He claimed the Aztecs came originally from Aztlan, the same place as the Toltecs. Legends say that Huitzilopochtli (right) told them to settle where they found the eagle.

FIERCE BEAUTY

In some ways the Aztec culture was colorful and beautiful. But it was also bloody. This turquoise mask, for example, is beautifully made. But it had a dark purpose. It was used in an Aztec religious ceremony. The person who wore it was probably sacrificed and eaten!

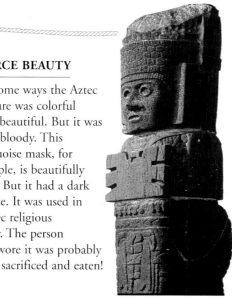

TOLTEC TEMPLES

When the Aztecs entered present-day Mexico, they found the remains of past civilizations. They discovered Toltec temple ruins, which contained huge statues. The one shown here is from Tula, the Toltec capital. Such architecture amazed the Aztecs. They decided to copy the ways of these ancient peoples. In 1427 they asked Izcoatl, a local prince who claimed to be descended from the Toltecs, to be their ruler.

AZTEC EMPIRE SPREADS

The Aztecs liked to pretend that they had a great empire. In truth, they were never all-powerful. They ruled with the help of two other cities, Texcoco and Tlacopan. These allies had helped the Aztecs conquer Tenochtitlan in the first place. There were some towns that the Aztecs never conquered. This picture shows warriors from Tlaxcala beating back the Aztecs in hand-to-hand combat. When the Spanish arrived in 1519, Tlaxcala was more than ready to join forces with them against their long-time enemy, the Aztecs.

THE AZTEC EMPIRE

This map shows the Aztec Empire at its height. The Aztecs ruled directly over the Valley of Mexico around Tenochtitlan. They also held power over surrounding tribes. The Aztecs allowed tribal leaders to rule over their own people. But they demanded large tributes (payments) from them in exchange.

Teotihuacan
Tula
Tlaxcala
Tlacopan
Tenochtitlan
Texcoco

Aztec Empire
Lake

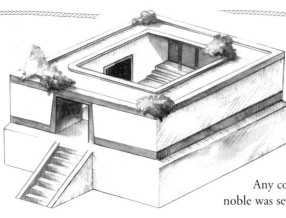

A NOBLEMAN'S HOUSE

The ruler, warriors, and nobles were the elite of Aztec society. Laws protected their special privileges. For example, only nobles could live in two-story houses. The nobles also lived closer to the center of the city than commoners. Any commoner who dared to pretend to be a noble was sentenced to death.

A LIFE OF HONOR

Not only did the laws protect the rights of nobles, they also set a high standard for behavior. There were strict laws against nobles who were unfaithful husbands or drunkards. Those who disobeyed the law would have to pay the price in the afterlife as well. This gold pendant shows Mictlantecuhtle, the lord of the dead. He was believed to rule the lands of misery beneath the earth. Souls who reached the land of Mictlantecuhtle were destroyed forever.

MONTEZUMA'S PALACE

This Aztec drawing shows Montezuma's palace in Tenochtitlan. It may look small in the drawing. But it was actually so large and complex that it was like a town of its own. The palace had different levels, or terraces. The top level was for Montezuma and his personal aides. The next level below was for his generals (left) and his advisers (right). Montezuma's officials worked hard. In return they were given fine houses and lands and were paid large salaries. In the Aztec Empire, only the nobles could become government officials.

Life for the Rich

The Aztecs conquered many cities, or at least threatened to do so. In return for not conquering a city, the Aztecs demanded tributes. Huge amounts of valuable goods flowed into Tenochtitlan. These included blankets, military outfits, beads, feathers, dyes, gold, cotton, peppers and spices, sacks of maize (corn), salt, and cacao beans. Some of these goods were used in public ceremonies. Some were given to nobles or to local merchants, who traded them for other goods.

MONTEZUMA II

In 1502 Montezuma II became the eighth high ruler of Tenochtitlan. He made sure no other person behaved as his equal. Nobles who went to see him had to take off their fine clothes and put on cheap blankets. They had to enter barefoot, with eyes cast down. They had to bow three times, saying: "My Lord, my great Lord!" When it was time to leave, they could not turn their backs on Montezuma. They had to walk out backward, eyes cast down again. Montezuma II ruled from 1502 until he was murdered in 1520, a year after the Spanish arrived.

A NOBLEMAN

Nobles were those who could trace their roots back to the Toltecs. Besides birth, the only other way to become a nobleman was to rise to a high position as a great warrior.

TRIBUTE ROLL

Tribute rolls showed the amount and type of taxes the provinces had to pay. The various symbols illustrated the type of goods that were to be sent to Tenochtitlan. At the height of their power, the Aztecs were receiving 200,000 tons of foodstuffs as tribute.

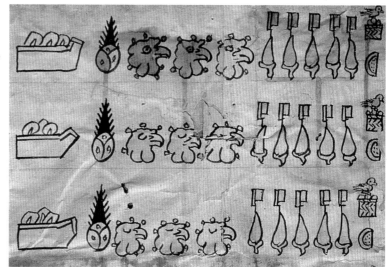

Life for the Poor

HOUSEHOLD GODS

Every home had a shrine that was a replica of the temple pyramids (see page 30) made from mounds of dough. The figurines above may have represented some of the 1,000 gods the Aztecs worshiped. Some statues were found with their heads broken off, which may have stood for victims who were sacrificed at the home shrine.

The poor and common folk of Aztec society were the lifeblood of the civilization. They lived at or near the bottom of the social ranks. The ruler was at the top, with the nobles below him. The citizens were below the nobles. They were organized into *calpulli* (groups) of about 100 families each. Each calpulli had its own area of the city. Each had a council of elders who kept records, shared out the land, and collected taxes. Most people stayed in the class into which they were born. Even lower than the citizens were tenant farmers and slaves. All three of these groups were the ones whose work made daily life possible for the Aztecs. They farmed, made goods of all kinds, built temples, and constructed causeways. Although these groups were low in rank, they were not thought to be inferior.

PEASANT HOUSING

About three of every four Aztecs were farmers. They lived in the countryside. Their houses looked like the one to the left. The huts had mud-brick walls and roofs thatched with leaves from maguey plants. They had no windows. As many as eight people lived in each one-room house. Some peasant homes had a flat roof. The rooftop served as an extra room.

SLAVES

This picture shows Chalchiuhtlicue, goddess of water, being waited on by slaves. Slaves were expensive. They cost as much as a person's expenses for a whole year. Slaves who could sing and dance well cost even more. Some slaves were given as tributes by conquered cities. Some were criminals whose punishment was to be made slaves. Sometimes peasants in debt would sell themselves into slavery for a loan to their family.

PEASANT POSSESSIONS

Poor families had few possessions. They used reed mats for beds and seats. Wooden chests held their few simple clothes. The center of their one-room homes was the hearth. Three stones arranged in a triangle supported the dish in which tortillas were made. Peasants also had digging sticks, brooms, baskets for keeping seeds, and hunting and fishing tools. Many also had a hanging cage in which a parrot or songbird chattered.

SIMPLE POTTERY

Even the poorest Aztec families needed pots. Every family had a water jar, a bowl for soaking maize, a flat grid for cooking, storage jars, plates, and cups. The three-legged bowl shown here, with its criss-cross ridges, was used for grating peppers.

A HARD LIFE

The common people worked hard. They paid taxes to keep up the temples and schools. In fact, half of Montezuma's income came from the commoners. The law set some limits on what ordinary people could do. For example, they could not wear fine clothes or build two-story houses. This peasant is wearing only a simple loincloth. For most Aztecs marriage, children, and honor were the true measures of a happy life.

Food & Drink

Maize was the mainstay of the Aztec diet. Aztecs were skilled farmers. They had no wheels, plows, or heavy animals to help prepare the soil. Aztecs used a simple digging stick, dropping one seed in each hole. For this reason, Aztecs preferred to farm the lighter soils. In the hills, the Aztecs built stone walls and created flat terraces for growing crops. In the hot valleys, they built aqueducts to bring water from the mountains. They even created farmland in the middle of a lake by creating islands called chinampas. The lake was also a good source of other foods, such as fish, frogs, and even insect eggs. Aztecs grew, caught, or traded for a wide range of foods, especially vegetables. Meat was scarce. Turkeys and hairless dogs fattened for the kill were the most common meats. Still, food was not plentiful. One Spanish writer noted that Aztecs ate "as little as anyone in the world."

FAVORITE FOODS

The Aztecs ate a surprising variety of foods. Favorites included kidney beans, sweet potatoes, avocados, maize, squash, peppers, tomatoes, mushrooms, duck, fish, rabbit, and snails.

DRINKING GOBLET

Drunkenness was a serious crime, even punishable by death. Old people, however, were allowed to have an alcoholic drink called *octli*, made from the maguey plant (see next page). The reasoning was that "their blood was turning cold." Those over 30 were allowed to drink about two goblets of octli on special occasions, such as weddings. Water was the regular drink of common people. Only the rich could afford *chocolatl*. This melt-in-the-mouth drink was made by boiling cacao beans and honey.

GROWING MAIZE

Maize was planted each May. In July, all but the best ears were picked from each plant. The full-grown cobs were harvested in September. The maize had to be soaked overnight to loosen the hull. Then it had to be boiled and skinned. Finally, it was ground down to flour and made into tortillas.

CHINAMPAS

The Aztecs turned the swamps near Tenochtitlan into farmland. They dredged mud from the bottom of the lake and piled it up to make fertile chinampas. Along the edges of these human-made islands, they grew willow trees to make strong banks. The trees' roots also anchored the islands.

MAGUEY PLANTS

The hardy maguey plant served many purposes. Its sap made a sweet syrup. The sap could also be fermented to make octli. The tough stem made good firewood and strong fence posts. The leaves fueled fires and stoves and provided thatching for roofs. The leaf fibers were used to make the rough cloth worn by the peasants. Rope, paper, sandals, nets, bags, and blankets were also made from the maguey plant.

FOOD FROM THE GODS

The colorful picture at the left shows Chicomecoatl, the goddess of corn, with one of her servants. In a planting festival in May, corn seed was blessed in her temple. At a September harvest festival, a priestess dressed as Chicomecoatl threw dried seeds at the crowds. People scrambled to catch these. Sacred seeds for the following year were then laid away in the temple of Chicomecoatl.

Pastimes

Every aspect of Aztec life had a religious meaning, even pastimes and games. Festivals and ceremonies played a very large part in everyday life. One of the Aztec calendars was divided into 18 months of 20 days each. There were festivals and ceremonies for each month. Most followed the seasons and centered on making the gods happy enough to send rain and good crops. Feasting, dancing, and singing were part of these festivals, as was human sacrifice.

CALENDAR CEREMONY

In this ceremony, four men dressed as birds. They attached themselves to ropes wound around a pole 13 times. Then they let go from the top and gradually unwound. The rope was measured so that they reached the ground in exactly 52 circles. This ceremony represented the union of the two Aztec calendars, which came together every 52 years.

AZTEC RHYTHMS

Most Aztec rhythm instruments were drums and rattles. The largest drum (second from left) was called the huehuetl. Its name, pronounced *way-waytl,* probably suggests how it sounded. People wore shells and seeds on their ankles, which shook in rhythm as they danced. The Aztecs also played flutes, and they used the conch shell as a horn.

CHILD'S PLAY

Aztec children were allowed to play with their toys, such as this pottery pull-toy, until they were about four years old. After that, they had to help with housework.

POETRY OF LIFE

This painting shows Xochipilli, god of music, **poetry**, **dance**, and flowers. In Nahuatl, the language of the Aztecs, *xochitl* means "**flower**." The Nahuatl word for *poetry* meant "flower-and-song." Most **Aztec poetry** was written to the god Tezcatlipoca ("Smoking Mirror"). He gave and took life. In many poems, flowers and song are linked with life and death:

> **You come out from the flower and song; You scatter the flowers, You destroy them.**

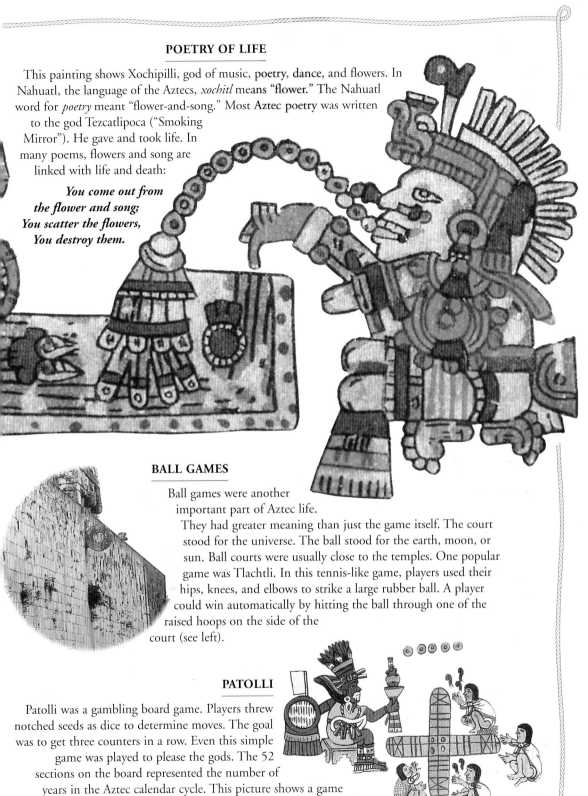

BALL GAMES

Ball games were another important part of Aztec life. They had greater meaning than just the game itself. The court stood for the universe. The ball stood for the earth, moon, or sun. Ball courts were usually close to the temples. One popular game was Tlachtli. In this tennis-like game, players used their hips, knees, and elbows to strike a large rubber ball. A player could win automatically by hitting the ball through one of the raised hoops on the side of the court (see left).

PATOLLI

Patolli was a gambling board game. Players threw notched seeds as dice to determine moves. The goal was to get three counters in a row. Even this simple game was played to please the gods. The 52 sections on the board represented the number of years in the Aztec calendar cycle. This picture shows a game being watched by Macuilxochitl, the god of plants and fun.

11

HAIRSTYLES

Aztec women usually wore their hair in two braids. These they brought around to the front of their heads and fastened together at the forehead. This statue of an Aztec goddess shows a different style. Her hair is gathered into bunches at the side of her head. She wears a braided headband. Young men shaved their hair, leaving only a pigtail at the back of the head. They could not cut off the pigtail until they captured a prisoner in battle.

MAKEUP MIRROR

This mirror is made of obsidian, a black volcanic glass. Women used it to see the effects of their dramatic makeup. They painted their faces and bodies with thick coats of red, yellow, blue, or green paint. Yellow skin was considered beautiful. So women rubbed their faces with a yellow cream made from crushed insects. They also stained their teeth bright red. Men also painted their bodies for some ceremonies.

NOBLE DRESS

Only a noble could dress like this. The colorful cotton cloak, decorated loincloth, sandals, and expensive necklace showed his status. Rich men sometimes wore layers of fine cloaks to show off.

FINE FEATHERS

Feathers were a vital part of a noble's dress. This picture shows Montezuma's headdress. The feathers were pushed into bamboo tubes. Then they were sewn together with a thread made of cactus fibers. Featherworking was an important Aztec industry.

Fashion

Strict laws determined what Aztecs could or could not wear. The common people were forbidden to wear colored cloaks, cotton cloth, or gold jewelry. The length of clothing was also set by law. If a man wore a robe of improper length, others would look at his legs. If these showed battle scars, the matter was dropped. But if they did not, he was put to death for dressing above his rank. Most poor men wore only a loincloth tied so that flaps hung in back and front. If they could afford a cloak, it had to be a rough, white blanket made from the maguey plant. A woman's basic dress was an ankle-length skirt and embroidered belt. A poncho-like blouse was worn over these. The poor usually went barefoot. The rich had leather sandals. A few even wore gold sandals.

COTTON VARIETY

Cotton had to be brought in from low-lying areas of Central America. It was soft and cool, an important fabric for nobles' clothes. Cotton was also used for bedding, bags, wall hangings, battle dress, and burial shrouds.

JEWELRY

Aztec nobles wore as much gold and jade jewelry as possible. They even wore nose plugs and pendants from their lips. The designs on this earring are a gold skull bone and tiny bells.

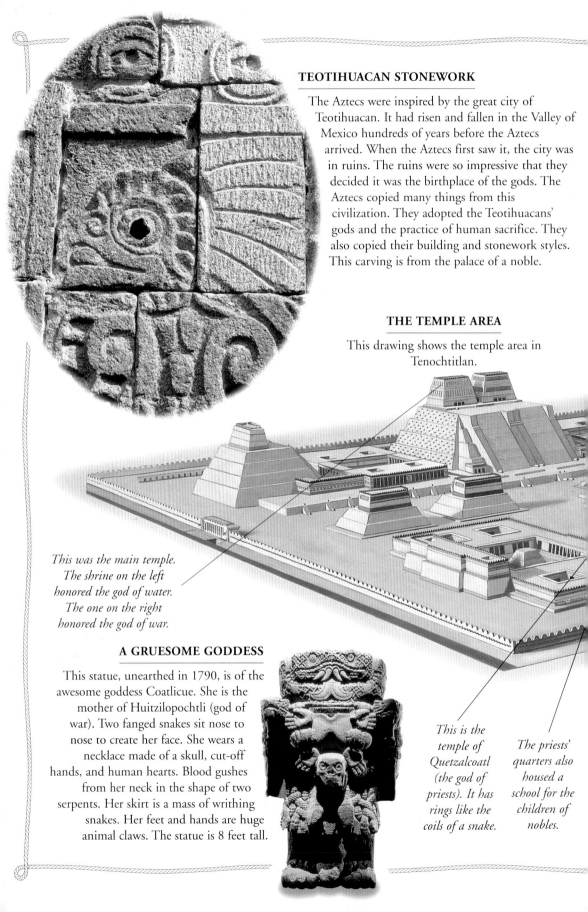

TEOTIHUACAN STONEWORK

The Aztecs were inspired by the great city of Teotihuacan. It had risen and fallen in the Valley of Mexico hundreds of years before the Aztecs arrived. When the Aztecs first saw it, the city was in ruins. The ruins were so impressive that they decided it was the birthplace of the gods. The Aztecs copied many things from this civilization. They adopted the Teotihuacans' gods and the practice of human sacrifice. They also copied their building and stonework styles. This carving is from the palace of a noble.

THE TEMPLE AREA

This drawing shows the temple area in Tenochtitlan.

This was the main temple. The shrine on the left honored the god of water. The one on the right honored the god of war.

A GRUESOME GODDESS

This statue, unearthed in 1790, is of the awesome goddess Coatlicue. She is the mother of Huitzilopochtli (god of war). Two fanged snakes sit nose to nose to create her face. She wears a necklace made of a skull, cut-off hands, and human hearts. Blood gushes from her neck in the shape of two serpents. Her skirt is a mass of writhing snakes. Her feet and hands are huge animal claws. The statue is 8 feet tall.

This is the temple of Quetzalcoatl (the god of priests). It has rings like the coils of a snake.

The priests' quarters also housed a school for the children of nobles.

Art & Architecture

Using only a simple wooden wedge driven into cracks, Aztecs could cut 40-ton slabs of rock. Teams of workers dragged the slabs to a building site. There they used metal chisels to decorate them.

Like other aspects of Aztec life, art and architecture served a religious purpose. The power of the gods was a repeating theme in Aztec art, especially sculpture. The grand temples were also built to honor and please the gods. Aztecs believed Tenochtitlan was the center of the earth. The city was carefully laid out on a grid pattern. The main street ran east to west, to mirror the passage of the sun across the sky. The temple area in the center of the city was especially grand. There were many fine buildings crafted with skilled stonework and woodwork. The wall surrounding this area was fashioned in the shape of wriggling snakes. Tenochtitlan was the most dazzling city in North America at its time.

This small platform was for a different kind of sacrifice. A captured warrior would be tied there and given a wooden club. A fully-armed Aztec warrior would then fight him to the death.

The skull rack was next to the ball court. One observer noted that the rack held 136,000 skulls of sacrificed victims.

The ball court was next to the temple of Quetzalcoatl.

GRASSHOPPER

This grasshopper was a symbol of Chapultepec ("Grasshopper Hill"), just north of Tenochtitlan. The artist is unknown. Artists did not sign their names to their work. They offered all of the credit and glory to the gods.

Health & Medicine

For the Aztecs, medicine was a mix of religion, magic, and cures from plants. On the whole, Aztec cities were cleaner and less crowded than other cities of the time. So disease did not spread as easily. The Aztecs also practiced personal hygiene. They washed often. They even took steam baths. They polished their teeth with a mix of salt and powdered charcoal to prevent decay. Aztecs called on doctors to treat people with illnesses. Some sickness was believed to come from outside the body, on the winds of a displeased god, for example. To know which god to appease, the doctors sometimes gave their patients a drug that caused visions. They hoped the patient would see the god and identify him or her. Doctors also used their knowledge of the healing power of plants to return a patient to health. They knew how to set broken bones. When they set bones, they also recited a magic spell for healing.

AZTEC DOCTORS

Aztec doctors knew how to be dramatic. They often brought ritual items, such as eagle wings, shells, and tobacco, to aid the cure. Sometimes they pretended to find and remove a stone dart, the carrier of the illness.

THE ROLE OF THE GODS

Pictured here is Tlaloc, the god of water. Aztecs thought he sent diseases, such as leprosy and ulcers, on the cold winds. Other gods were thought to be helpful in healing. Sick children were given water from the temple of Ixtlilton to help them recover.

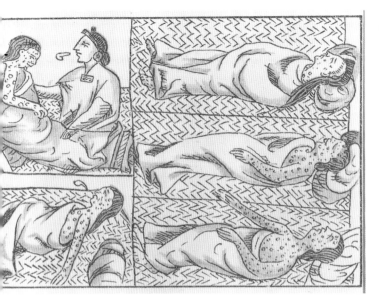

SMALLPOX

When the Spaniards came to Mexico, they brought new diseases with them. The Aztecs had no immunity to these diseases. The most serious was smallpox. Millions of Aztecs died of smallpox.

MEDICINE FROM PLANTS AND INSECTS

A good Aztec doctor knew how to use more than 1,500 herbal medicines. Doctors used different plants to bring down fevers, cure stomachaches, stop bleeding, and treat skin problems. Sometimes they added crushed insects to the mixtures.

FATES IN THE CRADLE

The Aztecs believed the fate of a child depended on the day it was born. The unluckiest days were the five days each year that did not fit into the 18-month calendar. This picture shows Chalchiuhtlicue, the goddess of clean water and childbirth.

MAGICAL CURES

Aztecs used magic in medicine. Sometimes a bundle of strings was thrown on the ground. If the strings stayed together in a clump, the patient's chances for recovery were poor. Parents dropped morning dew in the nostrils of children with stuffy noses. Some sick children were held over a pool of water. If their reflection looked shadowy, that meant a spirit had taken away their breath.

Love & Marriage

TYING THE KNOT

On the day of her wedding, the girl's parents gave a feast. After bathing, the bride painted herself yellow and put on her wedding clothes. At night, the marriage party would set off for the groom's house. The matchmaker carried the bride on her back. At the groom's house, the couple sat on a reed mat. Then the matchmaker tied the bride's blouse to the groom's cloak as a symbol of their marriage.

Marriage was highly valued in Aztec life. In fact, unmarried men could not receive a share of land in their precincts. Marriages were arranged by the parents. A young man's family would send a matchmaker to a girl's family, expressing interest in a marriage. The girl's family would turn the request down at first, offering such polite reasons as, "Oh, your son is too good for my daughter." Everyone knew, however, that the refusal was just custom. A few weeks later, after several more approaches, the match would be arranged. So would the exchange of money and property within the two families. Men could take more than one wife as long as they could support them and any children. Women could marry only one man.

XOCHIQUETZAL

This is a statue of Xochiquetzal, the goddess of beauty and love. Although she stood for love, she had a dark side too. She was believed to send boils to anybody who offended her. Those who indulged in bodily pleasure at the expense of other virtues were punished. According to legend, Xochiquetzal herself was thrown out of heaven for this offense. In misery, she gazed up at heaven and became blind with crying. The Aztecs believed this story explained why people cannot look at the sun.

MARRIED COUPLES

This picture shows a couple sharing the work of storing maize. Women and men had separate roles in a family. The women's roles were not thought to be less important. But women were advised by their elders to obey their husbands "cheerfully." Both men and women could request a divorce. If a husband deserted or harmed a wife, she could get half of the couple's land and possessions in a divorce.

AZTEC WOMEN

Aztec women cleaned the house, made the meals, wove cloth, and looked after the children. Meal preparation alone took several hours a day. The maize had to be prepared fresh for each meal. Otherwise it would spoil. Sweeping was a sacred duty, tied to the purity of the gods.

NEW ARRIVALS

Most Aztec couples were happy and grew to love one another, even though their marriages had been arranged. A childless marriage, however, often ended in divorce. The arrival of a child was a source of great happiness. If it was a boy, he was greeted with the wish that he become a great warrior who would feed the sun with his enemies' blood. A girl was blessed with the wish that she spend her life doing housework. Birth celebrations lasted for several weeks.

Children

For the first several years of their lives, boys and girls followed similar paths. They stayed close to their mothers and enjoyed the toys and games of childhood. After that, boys were expected to learn their life skills from their fathers. Girls began to learn the household skills of grinding, cooking, and weaving. As they reached their teenage years, children went to public schools. Girls were taught how to sing and dance at religious festivals. Boys helped with construction work and trained to be soldiers. The sons of nobles went to advanced schools. There they learned about war and religion. But they also studied history, medicine, mathematics, the calendar, astrology, and law. Aztec education taught children to obey. They were taught to think like everyone else, not for themselves. No one was allowed to be different.

PUNISHMENTS

This father is punishing his son by holding him over a fire and forcing him to breathe the stinging fumes of burning peppers. The blue speech comma shows that the child is also getting a lecture about his behavior.

SYMBOLS

The Codex Mendoza was a collection of drawings about Aztec practices made for the viceroy of Spain. The illustrations in the Codex about bringing up children (page 21) use the following key to show age and food. The red counters represent the age of the child. The yellow chips illustrate the number of tortillas they were allowed to eat per day.

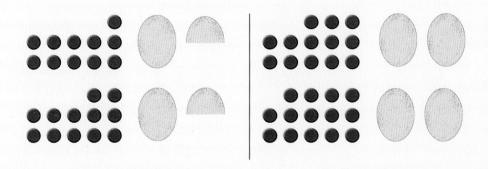

A BOY'S EDUCATION

Education for Aztec boys centered on learning skills they would need in later life. They also needed to be able to operate boats and canoes in order to work on the chinampas.

Here, a farmer is teaching his 12-year-old son how to carry loads and how to handle a canoe.

These were essential skills for a farmer when working on the chinampas.

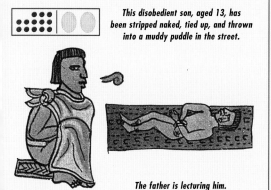

This disobedient son, aged 13, has been stripped naked, tied up, and thrown into a muddy puddle in the street.

The father is lecturing him.

This picture shows a farmer teaching his 14-year-old son how to fish.

At this age, the boy would have been eating two tortillas a day, so it was important that he earned his keep.

A GIRL'S EDUCATION

Most Aztec education for girls took place in the home. From an early age, a girl would be taught the skills she would use on a daily basis in her role as a homemaker in later life.

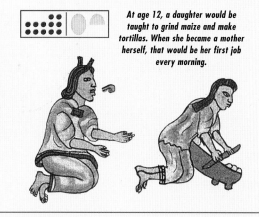

At age 12, a daughter would be taught to grind maize and make tortillas. When she became a mother herself, that would be her first job every morning.

At age 13, this girl is being taught how to sweep the floor. Sweeping was a vital religious duty.

Aztec women believed that when they swept up, they were helping the gods to purify the world.

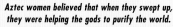

Weaving was a woman's job in the Aztec Empire. Here, the mother is teaching the 14-year-old girl how to use a backstrap loom.

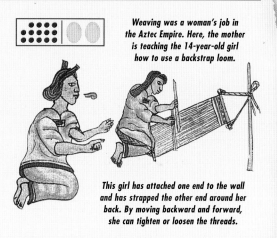

This girl has attached one end to the wall and has strapped the other end around her back. By moving backward and forward, she can tighten or loosen the threads.

War & Weaponry

The Aztec Empire fed on war. War provided the means for men to gain status in Aztec society. The more captives they took, the higher their rank. The captives were sacrificed to the heart-hungry gods. War also fed the economy. Tribute payments from conquered cities kept alive the bustle of Tenochtitlan. The Aztecs knew, however, that a destroyed city could not pay tributes. So when possible, they only threatened war. They gave their enemies several weeks to think over such threats. If the Aztecs' terms were accepted, the city usually could continue to govern itself as long as it paid its tributes.

A DEADLY CEREMONY

Capturing victims for sacrifice was a strong motive for going to war. As this Aztec painting shows, the captives in this ceremony were forced to dance all night. They were burned at the stake the next morning.

PROTECTION

This warrior's shield was made of wood covered with leather and decorated with feathers. Larger shields made of leather or wooden slats afforded head-to-toe protection and could be rolled up for storage.

DRESSED TO KILL

Aztecs had no standing army. Each precinct sent a regiment of men to fight as needed. Soldiers dressed as they liked, depending on their rank. All warriors, though, wore a thick quilted cotton bodysuit. It provided such good protection that some Spanish soldiers preferred it to their armor. This warrior's two-bladed club was so fierce it could cut off a head in one blow.

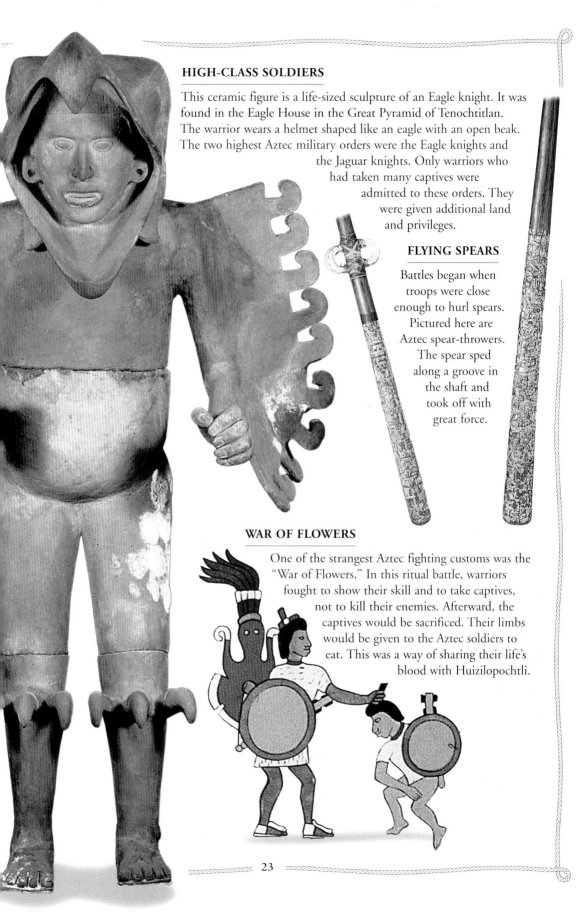

HIGH-CLASS SOLDIERS

This ceramic figure is a life-sized sculpture of an Eagle knight. It was found in the Eagle House in the Great Pyramid of Tenochtitlan. The warrior wears a helmet shaped like an eagle with an open beak. The two highest Aztec military orders were the Eagle knights and the Jaguar knights. Only warriors who had taken many captives were admitted to these orders. They were given additional land and privileges.

FLYING SPEARS

Battles began when troops were close enough to hurl spears. Pictured here are Aztec spear-throwers. The spear sped along a groove in the shaft and took off with great force.

WAR OF FLOWERS

One of the strangest Aztec fighting customs was the "War of Flowers." In this ritual battle, warriors fought to show their skill and to take captives, not to kill their enemies. Afterward, the captives would be sacrificed. Their limbs would be given to the Aztec soldiers to eat. This was a way of sharing their life's blood with Huizilopochtli.

Trade & Travel

In Aztec society, trade was considered sacred. It was an important way to keep the Aztec economy thriving. Merchants were treated almost like royalty in Aztec society. They paid no taxes. They had their own courts of law. They worshiped their own gods, including Yacatecuhtli, who protected roads and travelers. The merchants traveled as far south as present-day Nicaragua to bring in items for trade. Especially valued from the "hot lands" to the south were cotton, feathers, precious stones, chocolate, rubber, jaguar skins, and live birds. Merchants traded items made at home, such as copper mirrors, rabbit fur robes, and salt, for these goods. Each city had its own marketplace, and people loved to go there. As many as 60,000 people a day went to the great market of Tlatelolco.

MONEY BEANS

The Aztecs used cacao beans as money. They also used cotton cloaks, small copper bells, and quills packed with gold dust. Since cacao beans were used as money, only the richest could afford the delicious chocolate drink.

AZTEC SHOPPING

Twice a year, 371 cities under Aztec control sent tribute to Tenochtitlan. These goods helped the local markets thrive. This picture shows an Aztec market in Tlaxcala. In this market, as in others, items were arranged in an orderly way. There was an aisle for game animals, for example, and another for herbs. Slaves could be found in another section, cotton and fiber from the maguey plant in yet another. There were no set prices. People bartered for the goods. The marketplace must have been very noisy with all that bartering. Each market also had its own law court where disputes were settled and cheaters punished.

NOBLE TRANSPORT

The Aztecs had no horses. A common form of transport was the litter. Here, a person costumed like the god Xochipilli is being carried in a religious parade. Nobles and rich traders also used litters for short distances.

PORTERS

Trading trips could be dangerous. Traders had to cross borders into other states. They took weapons, sometimes even warriors, to protect themselves. If a trader was killed in a faraway land, he was given the same honorable death rite as a warrior. On these trading trips, everything had to be carried. Long trains of carriers, called porters, went along with the traders. They carried up to 60 pounds each. They wore head straps like the one in this carving to help them to bear the load.

CANOES

Canoes were vital for carrying heavy goods into Tenochtitlan. The canals formed the city's main "streets." Nearly everyone had a canoe. These dugout canoes were made from the largest tree trunks available. Destroying a trader's canoe was so serious that it was taken as a declaration of war. Citizens were not supposed to show off their wealth. On their return from trading trips, merchants would bring their goods secretly into the city at night by canoe.

LIZARD

SERPENT

EAGLE

RABBIT

WATER

DOG

MONKEY

GRASS

REED

OCELOT

Science & Technology

The Aztecs were creative in the ways that they served the gods. To make grand temples, they figured out how to extract and move huge blocks of stone with simple tools. They studied the heavens and learned much about astronomy. They created two calendars: The solar year had 18 months of 20 days each (the spare five days were considered unlucky); the sacred calendar had 260 days, with 20 months of 13 days each. Shown on these pages are the symbols they used for the 20 days of the sacred calender. The Aztecs also built aqueducts to bring in fresh water and broad causeways to connect the islands to the mainland.

AZTEC POTTERY

Some Aztec pottery makers were experts. They made pots like the one shown here, often painted with black. Most pottery was made by ordinary people as part of their day-to-day routines. Aztec potters did not use a wheel. Instead, they built up layers of rolled clay and shaped the pot with their fingers. Most of the pottery was very simple. Three-legged pots were very common.

ANIMAL MAGIC

Stonework was highly prized among the Aztecs. Montezuma even warred against certain cities to increase supplies of the sand used for polishing stones. Precious stones were used for jewelry and small carvings. This stone vessel is in the shape of a hare. Animals were favorite subjects for carvings.

CALENDAR STONE

The Aztecs believed there had been four failed worlds before the present age. They believed they were living in the age of the "fifth sun." This huge, 24-ton calendar stone (left) measures almost 12 feet (4 m) across. It shows the fifth sun, Tonatiuh, at the center. The four squares around the sun show the destruction of the four earlier worlds by jaguars, hurricanes, volcanic fires, and heavy rains. Pictures in the inner ring stand for the 20 days of the sacred calendar. Twisting beyond this ring are the two fire serpents. Their heads meet at the bottom of the circle.

THE LOST-WAX METHOD

Some gold jewelry was made using a technique called the "lost-wax" method. First, a model was made from charcoal and covered in beeswax. It was then coated in a paste of charcoal and clay. As hot metal was poured into the mold, the melted wax flowed out. The metal took its place in the desired shape.

THE NEW FIRE CEREMONY

Every 52 years the two Aztec calendars came together. The Aztecs believed this could cause the world to end. Five days before the end of the cycle, the Aztecs put out their fires, cleaned their homes, and smashed all their pots. On the fifth night priests dressed as the gods marched to a sacred hill. There, just as the star cluster Pleiades reached its highest point, a victim was sacrificed. A flame was lit where the victim's heart had been removed. From that spark a community bonfire was lit. Runners took torches from that fire to temples in other cities. The Aztecs believed that the ritual kept them safe for 52 more years.

VULTURE

FIRST KNIFE

FLOWER

HOUSE

RAIN

MOTION

CROCODILE

WIND

DEATH

DEER

Religion

THE GREAT TEMPLE

The Great Temple of Tenochtitlan kept getting greater, with seven additions over the years. By Montezuma's time, its base measured more than 270 feet (90 m) by 210 feet (70 m).

The Aztecs had a grim view of life. They saw life on earth as full of suffering, pain, and toil. Even after death, things did not always improve. People who died of disease or by accident went to the land of Tlaloc, a paradise where there was always spring. Everyone else had to endure terrible trials on the way to the underworld, where their souls were destroyed. Women who died in childbirth and great warriors fared better. They became gods who helped the sun to move across the heavens. After four years, warriors and victims of sacrifice came back to earth as butterflies or hummingbirds.

SPRING SACRIFICE

Aztec gods often hurt and helped people. Xipe Totec was a god of fertility and life. In sacrifices to this god, victims were shot with arrows. Their blood would "rain" down, bringing new life. Afterward, the Aztecs wore the victim's skin. This new skin stood for springtime's new growth. The god is often shown wearing the skin of a sacrifice victim.

THE COYOLXAUHQUI STONE

This stone was found at the foot of the stairs of the main temple. It shows the cut-up body of the moon goddess, Coyolxauhqui. She was said to have climbed a mountain to kill her mother as her mother was about to give birth to the god Huitzilopochtli. But Huitzilopochtli sprang out, cut his sister into pieces, and threw her down the mountain. This story explains why the bodies of sacrificed victims were thrown down the temple steps.

PRIESTS OF DEATH

Aztec priests painted their bodies black and wore long dark cloaks. Priests were forbidden to wash or cut their hair. They were expected to fast often and to bleed themselves. Priests' duties were to make sure that all ceremonies and sacrifices were performed correctly. They used knives like the one below to carry out sacrifices.

GIFTS TO GODS

The Aztecs believed that sacrifices were necessary to make the sun rise each day. Their gods demanded human hearts as payment. Huge numbers of victims were killed. Some sources say that more than 80,000 people were sacrificed at one ceremony alone.

RITES OF SACRIFICE

This picture shows an Aztec sacrifice. The Aztecs sacrificed people in many different ways. In one rite, a young man pretended to be the god Tezcatlipoca for a year. He was given everything he desired. He was taught noble ways and learned how to play the flute. At the end of that year he climbed the temple steps and his heart was cut out.

Another young man was chosen right away as next year's victim. On another occasion, captives were dusted with a pain-killing herb. Then they were thrown into a fire.

Legacy of the Past

MEXICAN FLAG

Mexico City was built on the ruins of Tenochtitlan. The Mexican flag bears the Aztec symbol of the eagle on the cactus.

The Aztecs were fearless warriors and great builders. Only the Inca in Peru created a larger empire. Aztec society was very well organized, with extensive trading networks. Aztec accomplishments in building, language, stonework, feather work, and other arts were also impressive. However, the Aztecs were fierce invaders who stole the heritage and ideas of the peoples they conquered. Their technology was primitive. They terrorized surrounding cities and sacrificed victims on a grand scale. The Spanish conquerors wiped out much of the Aztec legacy. But it is still possible to find elements of the Aztec way of life in their modern day descendants, the Nahua.

HISTORICAL HOUSES

Many of the Aztecs' descendants still live in thatched, mud-brick cottages like those of their ancestors. They cook in traditional ways and make traditional crafts. More than a million people speak Nahuatl, the language of the Aztecs. Nineteen out of every 20 modern-day Mexicans have some Aztec blood in their veins.

AZTEC PYRAMIDS

This is the Aztec Pyramid of the Sun at Teotihuacan. On certain days of the year, the moving shadows of the setting sun make the pyramid appear to wriggle. The Aztecs believed this showed the movement of their snake-god, Quetzalcoatl.

THE FALL OF THE AZTECS

On Good Friday in 1519, Hernán Cortés and 600 Spaniards landed on the coast of Mexico. Just three years later, the Aztec Empire had surrendered, and the city of Tenochtitlan lay in ruins. Aztec weapons and battle tactics were no match for the Spaniards. The Spaniards also won the help of the Aztecs' many enemies. When the conquest was complete, the Aztecs felt their gods no longer supported them. The Spaniards destroyed everything. They even set fire to a beautiful aviary. All the birds in it were killed in the fire. For many, many years the Spanish rulers kept Aztec artworks hidden. They feared their striking power would reawaken the Aztec religion in the people.

A NEW RELIGION

The Spaniards quickly destroyed the Aztec religion. They spread the message of Christianity, their own religion. Many Aztecs were happy to worship a God who did not require constant sacrifice. They were taken with the idea that Jesus had sacrificed himself so that humankind need not die. Today, many Nahua are devoted Christians. Traces of the old gods still survive in some modern ceremonies. Marigolds, once used to honor Xochiquetzal, are now part of the Christian festival of All Souls Day.

PRONUNCIATION

This is how to say the names of the most popular Aztec gods:

Chalchiuhtlicue
(goddess of clean water and childbirth)
pronounced **Chal-chee-weet-lee-kway**
Chicomecoatl (goddess of corn)
pronounced **Chee-co-me-co-atl**
Coatlicue (lady of the serpent skirt)
pronounced **Co-at-lee-kway**
Coyolxauhqui (moon goddess)
pronounced **Coy-ol-show-kee**
Huitzilopochtli (god of war)
pronounced **Weet-zil-o-potch-tly**

Macuilxochitl (god of plants and fun)
pronounced **Ma-kweel-sho-chitl**
Mictlantecuhtle (lord of the dead)
pronounced **Meek-tlan-tay-coot-ly**
Quetzalcoatl (Feathered Serpent, god of priests, creator)
pronounced **Kayt-zal-co-atl**
Tezcatlipoca (giver and taker of life)
pronounced **Tez-cat-li-po-ca**
Tlaloc (god of water)
pronounced **Tlah-loc**
Tonatiuh (sun god)
pronounced **To-na-tee-oo**
Xipe Totec (god of spring and fertility)
pronounced **Shee-pay To-tec**
Xochipilli (god of music, poetry, dance and flowers)
pronounced **Sho-chee-pee-ly**
Xochiquetzal (goddess of beauty and love)
pronounced **Sho-chee-kay-tzall**
Yacatecuhtli (god of travelers)
pronounced **Ya-ca-tay-coot-ly**

ACKNOWLEDGMENTS

Artwork: John Alston and David Hobbs   Picture Research: Image Select
Published by Jamestown Publishers, a division of NTC/Contemporary Publishing Group, Inc.
4255 West Touhy Avenue Lincolnwood (Chicago), Illinois 60712-1975, U.S.A.
This edition © 2001α by NTC/Contemporary Publishing Group, Inc. ISBN 0-8092-9489-3
First published in Great Britain by ticktock Publishing Ltd., The Offices in the Square, Hadlow, Tonbridge, Kent, TN11 0DD.
© 1998 ticktock Publishing Ltd. All rights reserved.
No part of this publication may be reproduced, stored in a retrieval system, or transmitted in any form or by any means without
the prior written permission of the publisher. Printed in Hong Kong.

Picture Credits: t=top, b=bottom, c=center, l=left, r=right, IFC=inside front cover, OFC=outside front cover

AKG; 2/3c & OFC, 2tl, 8c, 8/9cb, 11cl, 14tl, 16bl, 17t, 19c, 22bl. Ancient Art & Architecture; 7br, 12tl, 18/19c, 29cl. Ann Ronan @ Image Select; 13tr.
Asia; 10cl. Corbis; 30/31c & OFC. Elizabeth Baquedane; 9r, 14b, 18tl, 21br, 22/23c, 24t, 24tl, 28c, 31cr. et archive;, 2bl, 3bc, 3br, 5br, 5tr, 6/7c, 7tr, 8bl, 9t
& OFC, 10br, 11br, 12tl, 13br, 15tl, 16tl & IFC, 17cl, 19t, 24/25, 32 & OFC, 28/29c, 31ct. Image Select; 4c, 5br, 20/21 all. Planet Earth Pictures; 27c.
Spectrum Colour Library; 8tl. Nick Saunders/Barbara Heller @ Werner Forman; 10cl. Werner Forman; 5c & 29br, 6bm, 10tl, 12ct, 12/13tl, 23cr, 24r, 26tl,
26b, 26/27c & OFC, 28bl, 30cl.

Every effort has been made to trace the copyright holders and we apologize in advance for any unintentional omissions.
We would be pleased to insert the appropriate acknowledgment in any subsequent edition of this publication.